After Image

ALSO BY JENNY GEORGE

asterisk (chapbook)

The Dream of Reason

After Image

Jenny George

COPPER CANYON PRESS

Port Townsend, Washington

Cover art: Yamamoto Masao, *A Box of Ku #613*

Copper Canyon Press is in residence at Fort Worden State Park
in Port Townsend, Washington, under the auspices of Centrum.
Centrum is a gathering place for artists and creative thinkers
from around the world, students of all ages and backgrounds,
and audiences seeking extraordinary cultural enrichment.

LIBRARY OF CONGRESS CATALOGING-IN-PUBLICATION DATA
Names: George, Jenny, author.
Title: After image / Jenny George.
Description: Port Townsend, Washington : Copper Canyon Press, 2024. |
    Summary: "A collection of poems by Jenny George"— Provided by publisher.
Identifiers: LCCN 2024013450 (print) | LCCN 2024013451 (ebook) |
    ISBN 9781556596957 (paperback) | ISBN 9781619323032 (epub)
Subjects: LCGFT: Poetry.
Classification: LCC PS3607.E66295 A69 2024 (print) |
    LCC PS3607.E66295 (ebook) | DDC 811/.6—dc23/eng/20240329
LC record available at https://lccn.loc.gov/2024013450
LC ebook record available at https://lccn.loc.gov/2024013451

9 8 7 6 5 4 3 2 FIRST PRINTING

COPPER CANYON PRESS
Post Office Box 271
Port Townsend, Washington 98368
www.coppercanyonpress.org

Contents

After Image

A bee moves among flowers,
touching them briefly:

Someone saying, *here, here.*

Quantum

A table. And on it a vase
of flowering quince branches.

But a table is only a joke the gods
are making: continuous motion
disguised as permanence,
as a "place."
Something to set a vase on.
Something you can wipe with a cloth.

The body is not a place.
You learned this when her body became a sound
your voice was trying to make.

Like the orchard in spring, frenzied
with humming bees
ferrying the gold grains
from tree to tree, the endless
sexual material—
What you think is form
is just a kind of trembling.

Ars Poetica

Over the hours spanning dead of night
and early dawn, her face
changed to a stone under the surface
of a bright, transparent stream.
I observed this
happening. Like sex—
one part of me always remains
utterly unmoved.

Someone brought cloths, a bowl of flowers.
Raised the windows.
A scent floated like opened liqueur.

Then the light turned strange
and silvered, as though the air
were sealing off something
still close at hand.
A chill entered the room.

Describe this, the language
said, as the sudden snow
began—

Eclipse

All the birds are ill. They flood the elms,
driven to roost by a noontime dusk.
The trees are full of eyes. One body blots out
another body. Isn't that how it works?
She died. It floats on my vision like a burn:
Hands folded like a bride. Dark cave
of the mouth, open—as if a great sound
were being drawn in. We were very tired.
We covered her in flowers as she cooled.
The crescent of her foot hung off the bed.
       Now the birds are quelled,
disturbed and quiet. A strange hour of silk
descends. They settle in the trees—
if not to sleep, then to obey the dark.

*

You become Not-you.
A postcard of snow.
They tell me you
are at "rest."
In the window's cold
rectangle: a rose arbor
shipwrecked in a white field.

Rain and Stars

A person can be removed. All evidence
points to it. And in the space
left behind—

It rained all night.
A heavy, even rain that added to the pond.

Now there are tiny fish
scissoring in the blackness.
New alphabets, not encased in anything—
these ripples of emergence,

silver darts
in a withdrawing sky.

Black Butterflies

Before the two men from the mortuary touched
her body, they put their hands into black silk gloves.
Four black butterflies stood on the white bedsheet.
Four black butterflies wove the sheet into a chrysalis
around her. They rested lightly on her—a giant mother—
pulsing slowly, signaling to one another
with silent wingbeats. Then the butterflies carried
the bound form out into the bright, etherizing light
of late spring. I thought: This is what life does, it bears away
the damaged and the dead. Now she is in the world
in a new way, like a baby drained of all suffering.
And now when I sleep, from time to time my eyes flicker
open: black iridescent creatures hover, drinking
the warm, heavy drops upwelling from the source.

Afterimage

In the photograph, she is wearing a white dress.
Eyelets all down the front: little weepholes.
She is standing under the blooming theater
of an apricot tree, looking out from her not-knowing,
her being-alive. A strong sunlight
draws out the dark from under both eyes.
Now, what occurred is inevitable.
Like a water jar filled to the brim with water,
not one drop of space exists for any other
eventuality. Each spring the fruit trees
stage this same party, white garlands shedding
their blossoms all over the garden.
What is going to happen? She would seize
my arm in the night. The story ends
with a wedding. Then everyone endures.

Intertidal

After a swim, the sea
still dropping off the ends of her hair,
she sits on the stones
squinting back at the huge
ragged music of it,
salt drying in white violets
on her sun-dark shoulders,
seaweed flung on the tide line
like necklaces buzzing with flies.

All desire fails in the end, like the sea
repeating itself
against the same place, only to keep
changing it, leaving it diminished . . .

There once was a woman—
There once was a girl—

Oh, darling

All that is in the past now.
The dead live
in clear pools, inside language.

Eurydice

It snowed the day I died, a freak spring storm.
(It was in the papers.) A whole year of fruit was lost,
each snowflake traveling down from space
to touch a blossom with its cold crystal.
Now it's nearly spring again and inside the house
the one I married is forcing quince branches
in a jar of warm water. Oh, to be chosen, given a vessel,
shaped by another's strictures and desire! In the end
what do any of us want? Having been woken early,
brought into the human world and made to respond,
the little buds swell with their new circumstance.
The air is dense with invisible paths. That shock of fullness?
That's called life. That stab of light is the morning sun.

One Glove

I find a single glove in the winter box,
curled, emptied, like an unchanging hand,
a button at the wrist shining like a pill.
A lone glove suffers the other. It implies
the negative. Dusk arrives, a large room
with my house inside it, and my garden
bedded under straw for the season,
and the sound of the loons calling
from the pond. Where do they go
when they go away from here? Maybe
they are talking to each other in the dark
as they wait for instructions to rise in them
for travel to that distant place.

Black Dress

I see your clothes laid out on a bed:
an elegant dress like a soft skin
waiting for you to enter it
and go out.

Even from here I can see
the fabric is soft, a rich damask.
If you've left your dress on the bed   your body
must be close by.

A larva enters a cocoon, emerges—

Big butterfly with soot-black wings,
a newspaper opening and closing,
rustling, telling the news.

Snowstorm, April 28

You were not dead.
How could you be
when never once
before in all this
time had you
been other than
alive, and famously?
A fury of snow.
You were not dead.
The air a world
of cold white bees.

Kitchen Shears

Afterward, I cut the T-shirt off her.
I used the kitchen shears
which had previously been used
to make lengths of rosemary
as a bed for fish.

I cut the shirt crookedly
not from haste but because
my hands were executing
an entirely new gesture.
The cloth came free at her throat.

Outside, a low cloudcover had gathered.
I wrapped a fresh sheet around her.
I folded her hands on her chest
where they hardened, a plate of armor
against the living.

Orpheus in the Garden

I'm on my knees again
planting hard peas
like a row of tiny brains.
I drive each one deep
into the cold obstruction.

Afterlife

The apricot tree will bear
no apricots this year.
In early spring a shudder
of blossoms came over it briefly,
but another severe night arrived,
leaving ice in the pail.
By morning, the tree was stripped.

A personhood flashes through me:
something electrical
and bright
through my limbs.

Like a sudden impulse
to speak
or to knock someone down.

The Problem of the Lantern

The dead are difficult.
One of them was looking at me last night
from the hallway. Although *seeing* me, I don't know.
There was a quality like unmoving pondwater.
And a peculiar gleam like a false dawn.
The dead are not personal. That is part of the difficulty.
Like the problem of the lantern:
It illuminates without seeing, unless seeing
is itself the element that falls on things
in the form of light.
I often lie awake in the dark for hours.
Death is a brand-new experience, but it's not clear
who it happens to.

Mythology

They say one breast gives milk, the other honey—
But no god appears in my garden—that's just the sun
filtered through trees. Another day arriving
disguised as today. The fountain gurgles with water.
Insect-noise grows like the song of a single head.
Bees are already making use of the day, droning paths
through air, coming to drink on the wet stones.
They polish their faces like little hand mirrors.
The sun climbs the sky. Once I stood naked
in a garden eating pancakes smeared with apricot jam.
It was like being born—the space between two notes
of a struck bell, my whole body thrillingly separate
from my mind. Love, if you're real, make me
the earth's again. Lie down with me on the grass.

Jenny George

Is a failure in the garden.
Wherever she makes a hole
the earth slides back in urgently.
Seeds won't sprout for her; they won't
produce their yellow tongues.
There's just a voice saying, *No—I refuse to be born*
out of nothing. Even so, she keeps
making the dark trenches.
Ants overcrowd the buds of her peonies.
All is on its knees.
A small wind deranges the serviceberry.

Someone should help Jenny George.
When the sun goes behind the hills
there will be no one left
who knows who she is.

Form and Feeling

Suddenly I was in our house again.
Someone was telephoning about the removal.

It will all be handled. Good, good.

Turns out a one-person sailboat
had been stranded
in the doorjamb between
the bedroom and the hall.
It would need to be angled just right
to navigate the predicament.

A downed sail lay whitely over the skiff.
A smell began to bloom
beneath the wood. The sea
had all drained away.

And if the experts don't arrive?
Will living have to encompass this?

Migration

Crows assemble in the bare elm above our house.
Restless, staring: like souls
who want back in life.

—And who wouldn't want again
the hot bath after hard work,
with soft canyons of splitting foam;
or the glass of spring water
kissed to the mouth?

To be startled by beauty—drops of bright
blood on the snow.
To be radiant.

All morning the crows watch me in the garden
putting in the early onions.
Their bodies look oiled.
Back in, back in,
they shake the wooden rattles.

The Head of Orpheus

okay okay I am being carried along on a great river
I pass through the country through fields alongside
ruins and orchards I ride like a cup on a saucer
the river is a large continual motion that isn't me

I hear light vibrating in my mouth a heart
beats inside this head apparently something is singing
fragmented music trails me a foam of moments
a flicker of tree-shadow touches my face
touch without sensation

of my prior existence I have only a phantom
knowledge did we love did we lie down
among the bee-sound on warm grass
a head is only now now now

The Kindnesses of Death

First, that nothing touches you.
No silks unnerve your skin. No sunlight
splashes your empty face.

Next, that you cannot hear
the separations in the cries of birds.

At last all things stop changing: the wind
stays undisturbed in its enclosure.
No hour grows long with awful feeling.

That others are released from love.
No one has to bathe you now
like a worn-out child . . .

The kindnesses
fall down on you like steady snow.
Under which you always
neither sleep nor don't.

Nap

When I fall asleep in the afternoon
I see myself from the outside.
A life is just a large, toppled flower
floating on a pond. I think—So this is what
we all come down to: an occurrence
of bizarre gentleness, drifting
through spearshafts of light.
The flower transfers to me its emptiness.
Then the self is in the body again,
my face hot on the pillow, a hornet
nudging the upper corner of the room
with the sound of a small machine.

Sunflowers

I'm in the world but I still want the world.
I'm full of longing and can't move,
enthralled in the garden. Having died
all the way back to the root, I grow again
into a version of the thing I love. I'm her
and not her, hermaphrodite with a heart
like a plateful of black flames.
The bees inspect me like doctors.
All my hard little tears, future selves
who haven't grown. Bedclothes swell on the line.
Around me giant sunflowers burn
through their masks of radiant desire.

Carrier Bag

I have a new job which is to gather items
and collect them in this sack called life.
But there are holes in the sack and you
are one. Like a crack in a meadow—
a place where grasses aren't.
Or wild daisies. Or spring willows
whose cool furred buds are like strands
of sealskin pearls. I touch what isn't you.
I put everything in the sack.
Corpses, thunder, snakes copulating
in a ball. I put everything in.
And some things leave through the holes
and some things are too big to leave.

Civility

And what was it like after the furies
went underground?

On a breezy summer evening
we dined outside, the corners of the table weighted
with little solid silver rabbits.
A draining light caught the treetops.

At dusk the moon rose and briefly entered the pond.

We had apricots glazed in good wine, spooned out
clear as birdsong
onto individual dishes.

We had our civility. To demonstrate
we stroked the little silver rabbits gently
between their silver eyes.

Vivarium

Some people collect dirt from significant places.
Or spoonfuls of cloudy ocean inside jars.
Like amateur naturalists, they keep
these treasures permanently on a shelf.
Of course an amateur is simply a person
who loves, who brings love to bear
on a particular subject.
Returning from one trip I failed to bring back
a jar of anything. I stood outside my house
where white stitches of snow were dissolving
into the ground beneath the evergreens.
An unset moon floated over the trees.
If I stand very still, I do no further harm.
I am a tiny theater of non-harming. My breath
watches raptly. Sees how everything is still alive.

The First Strangers

The first lovers were the first strangers.
They had the first faces, appearing to one another
like the moon in lake water.

They were the first to speak.
The first to touch.

They stood in the orchard,
in all that had not transformed.
Soon the fruit trees would be foaming up from black fissures.

They belonged to nothing.
Instead of childhoods they had the snow. They simply walked
out of the origins of themselves.

The first losses accumulated between them.
And the first of many microscopic acts of attention, all unrecorded,
all swept into the birthplace of ashes.

To each the other was an infinite stranger.
So she took the bread from her own mouth to feed her.
She took the bread from her own mouth to feed her.

I Love You

Her eyes were mostly shut. She didn't speak.
The sun's slow exile crossed the wall above the bed.

But once, when I bent to feed her a drop
of morphine from the little plastic beak,

her hand shot up and gripped my arm. She looked right at me.
When she said the words, it sounded like she meant: *Don't leave me.*

From the very first, we love like this: our heads turning
toward whatever mothers us, our mouths urgent

for the taste of our name.

Spring

I hate
my grief. The way it keeps
repeating the same
question over and over.

At wood's edge the crows congregate
in large numbers to sleep.
When the sun appears, it sets off the great exchange.

Melt-pools flash. Her perfume bottles,
unmoved on the bureau, glow like glass fruit.

Two Rabbits

I was carrying a rabbit.
Abruptly it became two rabbits,
each one half the size of the original.
They throbbed in my hands.
Their fur was fresh and soft.

This had happened once before,
when my life first split
into *comfort* and *pain.* Now
with my coat flapping, I was carrying
the two rabbits across an autumn field.
In the distance: a lamplit house.

The days were getting increasingly smaller,
each day climbing out of the one
before, uncomprehending.

Untitled

You were showing me your new
                              white dress . . .

I wake to fresh snow. The woods
are giving off a low light, as though overnight
an aspect of their nature has been unconcealed.
The house is banked in quiet. You die each day.

Jenny George

Is not to be trusted. She will tell you
The soul narrows until it is just the breath.
She will call it *a violent narrowing.*
But her words are just images gleaned
off a dying girl like an apple peel
pared in a slow spiral off an apple.
She herself has never passed through
that hollow reed. An *unreliable narrator*
they used to call it in the seminars.

There are things you simply can't know
until you have lived through them.

At any rate, strangers now wear the girl's clothes
on the streets—the very streets
she and Jenny George would walk
with ice creams melting over their hands.
Or while a slew of blossoms
gusted suddenly through that corridor.

You might see a red dress crossing
in the crosswalk. The hem of it billowing.

Eurydice

Today I wandered around
my life, seeing the little agonies,
each one touched by pleasure
as though by a beam of sun.
Do I have these right—agonies, pleasure?
I could almost feel a light wind
moving the curtains.
I saw that all of this was drafts of paper
sailing off the surface of a table,
getting mixed up
and born. The dead are the ones
who really love, but then
only in retrospect. Birds flinging drops
from a sun-splashed fountain. Great golden cities.
Gemlike berries underneath the leaves.

Mushroom Season

A week of rain.
Then overnight a crop of mushrooms appears by the woodpile,
pale and luminous, the largest one like a hand
pointing out of the earth.
Fog drips from the trees. The air is lush
with cold urges.

Everything has a voice,
even if low, diffuse—or
outside human hearing.
And what doesn't speak
appears as signal:
sent up from the giant tracts
of the underworld,

silver thread-silk fine as hair,
creature without eyes or mind—

Fruited, rain-fed, variant, seeping

Moons, velvets, small grave-pearls, trumpets, milk

Here

A moth is desiccating
on our bedroom windowsill,
over days becoming
freed of its luster,
its moon oils
turning to a kind of powder
bound together
by duration.
The house is silent.
One year dead, you are
far away somewhere
with your new gift.
I wait on our bed,
the curtains moving slightly
as if from a hand.
Evening comes on.

Where does it hurt, they ask.
Where, specifically.

The Head of Orpheus

Like the bees who move violently, all at once
from the hive—

You find them suspended
from a tree in a furious ball
of low-throated humming.

They are trying to make a new body.

The Living

The earth goes on without me.
It's humiliating.
Peony shoots pushing their purple faces
out of the ground;
creak and rub of young apricot limbs in wind.
The *living* everything is doing. While I,
in my strange agency, am not even
somewhere.

The seasons keep changing into each other;
big shadows of clouds move
with coolness and with blushing
over the meadow grass.

I do not accommodate it.
I do not bless you. You
who are trying to say this.

The Artist

A snake lies in the open, dormant
in its sleeve of heat. A gilded orphan
on the sun-warmed dirt, eye-slits ajar,
waiting for the infinite to arrive.
You want to strike it with a stick.
You want an answer to the prayer
that says, *Make use of me.*
One day the old life simply sheds
its dress and flows through the stones.
Then the future wavers up in you
and stands in your throat like a flame.

Autobiography of a Vulture

I hatched from the void.
Crawled into the glow
on my pinhooks, craving meat.
The first scrap unlocked my throat.
All of us in the nest
open and swaying for it—
little death flowers.

Days, the sun was extreme
and mothering.
At night, the moon's head
rose over the hills.

—

With time, talent came into my wings.
And my eyes grew deep
inside my hood.

Everywhere I looked
I saw a body's helplessness, its need
to lie on the earth.

I followed my hungers
across the open fields.

—

I know I am reviled.
When you see me, you think of violence,
of deprivation—

I find death where it is:
simultaneous with life.
Bit by bit, I transfigure it.
Shreds of skin, pliant organs
of the interior.
My rancid stomach digests it all
like a little stove.
Until what's left is just
the bones, the silent ancestors
enduring in the grass.

—

I, who am tenant of the partition—
clawed by wind, existing
in the golden needles of the grasses—
I stand with the dead.

At the field's edge, with all
who have rotted and who will,

I stand griefless in my black overcoat.

Hello World

Someone gave me this: a body.
Big disappointing
form I cannot control.
I attach to it
a series of names.
I tend the garden of immediate decay.
Comb the strange stars from its hair.
My lungs inherit the weather
through an open window.
How am I supposed to
keep at this difficult task?
Life lasts so long now.

Anniversary

Abruptly awake. The room
moon-occupied, unfamiliar.
Whatever *it* is, it can disappear.

Over time the sun seeps in, an opened yolk.
A growing eye
takes in paint-peeled boards. A table with chairs.

Now the birds are our marriage.
I put the seeds out
every morning
on a white plate.

August

You know you will die, of course you do.
But you picture it as a place you've been before,
perhaps many years ago, as a child.
Old floorboards worn smooth, punctuated by nails.
The corner desk with all the small drawers.

The others are here somewhere too. In the kitchen,
or out on the porch.

A meadow slopes down to the lake, with a path mowed through it.
In the daytime, yellow butterflies blink over the grass.
At night, the moon
closer than you've ever seen—
And the bedsheets holding a faint odor of the lake.

You think of it like this. Like some version of the past,
but lasting a very long time.

You imagine you're ready. You have
your little shovel and pail.

Fortune

Autumn, with its vivid exchanges,
streams the avenues
of an old city. The falling leaves
produce a kind of wedding.
There's a thinness to the air.
Golden cottonwoods tremble with their visions.

We walk along the street
with our shoulders nearly
touching. One of us
carries a bag of delicate pastries
wrapped in paper like sticky jewels.

Here, says the Future, that famous comic.
Here are your lives. They are yours
to live in extravagantly.

The Late Days

Heat. Heat
and no rain. Days accumulate
like blankets.
The riverbed is just a fracture.

Then, this morning: an hour
of fall, breathing through the restless cottonwood trees—
a mother in the hallway
with a cool cloth to lay against this fever.
The earth tilts.

Oh, where are you?
I hurt you and I need
you. I'm a human child.

Address me.
Soothe me while I burn
you down.

The Lovers

The dead turn toward us
the face we turn toward them.
In this they are unified.
Like the earth, absorbing everything.
Aboveground the living
continuously merge and separate.
In the trampled grass
a few strewn petals of garbage . . .
            The breath
of the wind stirring these locust trees.

7 lb. 14 oz.

They burned you down to a box
and gave you back
to me like that—newborn dust,
your exact birthweight's
worth—now wrapped in a black
velvet bag and delivered
into my remaining hands.

The Lions

You can't take them with you,
they said to you at the crossing.
You can't
take anything.

Now I have your lions.
I feel the warm breaths venting off them.
A large stillness watches me
from the alien rooms of their eyes.
When I walk into the orchard
they follow me as far as the trees.

Atonement

I stood in a lamplit kitchen
looking into my empty life.
Outside, moths grazed the windowscreens
like tiny winged horses.

I had lived so close
to my life I could almost
feel it: it hummed
like an electric fence.
Often I had been afraid,
standing motionless at the edge.

Forgive me, I sang to the life.
How beautiful, how painful you almost were,
I sang with my burning
inaudible voice.

Memory

Looking up at me from her bath
she said, *Remember
everything we ever did?* A garland
of bones down her back.

Interior (winter morning)

Sunlight decants from the other half
of existence into this one.
In the kitchen, a bowl of mandarins
radiates emptiness.
                              Who were you
that even now the air's disturbed?
Steam twists from the kettle.
The body goes on living
while the self tunnels away
at its voluminous dream, a vole in snow.

The Hero

The hero who fails is still
a hero. Like the inverse
of a great problem: also great.

Late afternoon, the sun through pines
is making stabs at love. The light's minor
key. I go walking alone in the forest

as in all the old tales
where the vault beneath certainty opens.
Far off, a woodpecker's dense hammering.
The sinking sun makes a house of shafts.

All my life I have carried my solitude
like a jar of ashes. Suddenly someone
adjusts the lens of the microscope and the forest swells
with light. I leap toward you.

Orpheus Ascending

A crack appeared.
Beyond it, snow was pouring through the spring sunlight.
A bright, dry snow
like particles of unearthly metal.

I emerged.
And the earth closed after me, keeping her inside,
the way an instrument case
will seal shut around its black music.

Or was I the instrument?

Or was it not music, but pain
singing from the depths?

———

Aboveground
the peonies were smothered
in snow, bent beyond their weight with ice-white.
The bare-root apple couldn't hold
and snapped. I kept looking back
to where the bed stood stripped
like a table.

———

Then came the smack of snowmelt
off the eaves, the house weeping and shining
under fresh sun.
Every water bucket brimmed.
The garden—rinsed, dismantled—
breathed out a new green.

And with all the windows open, through the space
came the sound of—what were they?
Meadowlarks?

Days elapsed, years.

———

I still live
in our little house by the orchard, sited so the setting sun
illuminates the garden,
the bubbling fountain
like a fountain of fire in the final moments
before night draws across its lid.
Then, absolute quiet.
Even the wind resting in the trees.

We on earth, how can we know
how long the silences will be
between the movements?

I wait for song
to grow in me across the dark interval.

Jenny George

Is writing about snow again.
An unseasonable, glittery, sudden, etc.
The words stick on the paper.
When she writes, *It snowed,* who
does she mean? *She snowed.*
The snow snowed. No one
takes responsibility these days.
Snowdrops spring up from the cool understory.
You can't look anywhere and not be
looking at the world exactly as it is.

First Snowdrop

White bone-bell emerging
from last year's broken
down leaves;

little cup of inverted
feeling

that begins in the dark

and on spring's signal
climbs out—

as if the instructions are:
to articulate.

January 1

Cold, clear morning in the new year.
A wood thrush hidden in the snow thicket
sends out her bit of music like a bell-note.
(I think "her" because of *her*.) I won't turn
to look for the source. The song suffices;
there's a being there. I'm old enough now
to know the bond of all things arising, that continual
stumbling forth—sound from the silence
that surrounds it, crimson berries on the snow;
this wood thrush, the clear atoms of her music,
only seeming to deviate from the whole. Listen,
I'll keep trying to love. As I cross the meadow,
sparks of wind drive the white surface
upward into the sunlight like traveling fires.

Tin Bucket

The world is not simple.
Anyone will tell you.
But have you ever washed a person's hair
over a tin bucket,
gently twisting the rope of it
to wring the water out?
At the end of everything,
dancers just use air as their material.
A voice keeps singing even
without an instrument.
You make your fingers into a comb.

Opening of the Mouth Ceremony

In early times
for this ritual they used
a sacred blade (I almost wrote *scared*)
made of bronze and shaped like two hooked fingers
to prepare the mouth for speech
in the afterlife.

They circled around
like bees working at a flower, doing their maneuvers.
A small tray held the necessary tools.

With the mouth open, the body abandons its need
for assertion.

Finally the hands were placed as guardians
on the chest. Coins lay on the eyes: gold leaves
floating on a dark pond.

It's silent now. I'm ready
for what hasn't happened yet.

Notes

"THE HEAD OF ORPHEUS"
In some versions of the myth, either wild beasts or maenads tear off Orpheus's head; the head remains intact, singing as it floats down a river before washing up on the island of Lesbos. The structure of "The Head of Orpheus" (okay okay I am being carried along) is inspired by "bon bon il est un pays" by Samuel Beckett.

"AUGUST" begins with a line recast from James Longenbach's poem "The Harbor."

Acknowledgments

Poems published in this book have appeared in Academy of American Poets Poem-a-Day, *The Adroit Journal, Copper Nickel, The Georgia Review, Granta, The Iowa Review, The Kenyon Review, Los Angeles Review of Books, The Massachusetts Review, Mississippi Review, Orion, Plough-shares, Plume, Poetry, The Poetry Review* (UK), and *Sixth Finch*. "Orpheus Ascending" first appeared in *The Map of Every Lilac Leaf: Poets Respond to the Smith College Museum of Art*. A number of poems first appeared in the chapbook *asterisk*, published by Bull City Press in 2023. Thank you to all the editors who gave this work a home.

Thank you to Lannan Foundation and MacDowell for giving me time and space to write these poems.

Gratitude to the writers and friends who accompanied me and offered invaluable support and wisdom as I worked on this book: Nancy Barickman, Kipp Bentley, Ellen Casey, Nubia Domres, Matt Donovan, Erik Ehn, Chloe Goodwin, Kay Hagan, Roxane Hopper, Piper Kapin, Anne Haven McDonnell, Carol Moldaw, Kim Parko, Supriya Lopez Pillai, Terri Rolland, Linda Running Bentley, Jenn Shapland, Nathan Naik Shara, Elaine Sullivan, Arthur Sze, and Ashley E. Wynter. Deep gratitude to Jan Arsenault. This book was conceived of and completed during a long, ongoing conversation with my sister, Madeleine George. I am forever grateful for her presence and insight.

About the Author

Jenny George is the author of a previous poetry collection, *The Dream of Reason.* She has received support from the Bread Loaf Writers' Conference, the Iowa Writers' Workshop, Lannan Foundation, MacDowell, and Yaddo. Her poems have appeared in *The Kenyon Review, The New York Times, Ploughshares, Poetry,* and elsewhere. She lives in Santa Fe, New Mexico, where she works in social justice philanthropy.

Poetry is vital to language and living. Since 1972, Copper Canyon Press has published extraordinary poetry from around the world to engage the imaginations and intellects of readers, writers, booksellers, librarians, teachers, students, and donors.

WE ARE GRATEFUL FOR THE MAJOR SUPPORT PROVIDED BY:

academy of
american poets

OFFICE OF ARTS & CULTURE
SEATTLE

ARTSFUND

THE PAUL G. ALLEN
FAMILY FOUNDATION

Hawthornden
Foundation

POETRY FOUNDATION

INGRAM
CONTENT GROUP

the point
envision·enact·evolve

MCSWEENEY'S

WASHINGTON STATE
ARTS COMMISSION

National
Endowment
for the Arts
arts.gov
ART WORKS.

The Witter Bynner Foundation
for Poetry

TO LEARN MORE ABOUT UNDERWRITING
COPPER CANYON PRESS TITLES,
PLEASE CALL 360-385-4925 EXT. 105

WE ARE GRATEFUL FOR THE MAJOR SUPPORT PROVIDED BY:

Anonymous

Jill Baker and Jeffrey Bishop

Anne and Geoffrey Barker

Donna Bellew

Will Blythe

John Branch

Diana Broze

John R. Cahill

Sarah J. Cavanaugh

Keith Cowan and Linda Walsh

Peter Currie

The Evans Family

Mimi Gardner Gates

Gull Industries Inc.
   on behalf of William True

Carolyn and Robert Hedin

David and Jane Hibbard

Bruce S. Kahn

Phil Kovacevich and Eric Wechsler

Maureen Lee and Mark Busto

Ellie Mathews and Carl Youngmann
   as The North Press

Larry Mawby and Lois Bahle

Petunia Charitable Fund and
   adviser Elizabeth Hebert

Suzanne Rapp and Mark Hamilton

Adam and Lynn Rauch

Emily and Dan Raymond

Joseph C. Roberts

Cynthia Sears

Kim and Jeff Seely

Tree Swenson

Julia Sze

Barbara and Charles Wright

In honor of C.D. Wright
   from Forrest Gander

Caleb Young as C. Young Creative

The dedicated interns and faithful
   volunteers of Copper Canyon Press

The pressmark for Copper Canyon Press
suggests entrance, connection, and interaction
while holding at its center
an attentive, dynamic space for poetry.

This book is set in Reminga Pro.
Book design by Gopa & Ted2, Inc.
Printed on archival-quality paper.